Teachers' Guide

Year 2

Story-writing
SCAFFOLDS

Written by
Frances Mackay

HOPSCOTCH EDUCATIONAL PUBLISHING

Published by Hopscotch
A division of MA Education Ltd
St Jude's Church, Dulwich Road
Herne Hill, London SE24 0PB
Tel: 020 7738 5454

Written by Frances Mackay
Series design by Blade Communications
Illustrated by Leonie Shearing
Cover illustrated by Kirsty Wilson
Printed in the UK by CLE, St Ives, Huntingdon, Cambridgeshire

ISBN 1-905390-27-0
ISBN 978-1-905390-27-4

Year 2

Story-writing
SCAFFOLDS

CONTENTS

Story-writing Scaffolds for Year 2

INTRODUCTION

Story-writing Scaffolds Year 2 is intended for use in schools to help teach children how to write effective short stories in a variety of different genres. It aims to improve the children's ability to organise their own writing. As they work through the units, the children assemble a portfolio of stories containing genre-specific vocabulary and writing features. The chosen text types correspond to those in the National Literacy Strategy's *Framework for teaching*.

The book is accompanied by six full colour fiction titles that are used in conjunction with each unit in the book. The six exemplar storybooks are:

- *A Present for Dad* by Roger Carr;
- *Johann and the Birds* by Sarah Prince;
- *The Elves and the Shoemaker* by Meg Stein;
- *The Ungrateful Tiger* by Julie Ellis;
- *Don't Worry!* by Christopher Stitt;
- *Lost in the Park* by Roger Carr.

(The six books are all part of the 'Alphakids' series published by Eleanor Curtain Publishing.)

Contents

This book contains six units – two for each term. Each unit contains:

- notes for teachers about each genre;
- guidance for teachers on the questions to ask and discussion ideas after reading the exemplar storybook;
- three photocopiable activity sheets to follow up the reading of the story;
- a wealth of further speaking and listening and writing ideas to carry out after reading the story;
- photocopiable differentiated story scaffolds;
- photocopiable differentiated word banks.

How to use the units in this book

1. Share the exemplar storybook with the children. The guidance notes for each unit provide suggestions for questions to ask the children after/during the reading. The notes also provide ideas for further discussion.
2. Use the three photocopiable activity pages for each unit to revisit the story with the children. These pages include comprehension, sequencing, grammar and punctuation activities. These pages may also provide you with ideas for developing your own activities.
3. If appropriate, select some activities from the further ideas section. There are enough ideas on these pages to carry out related work for several weeks.
4. Tell the children they are going to write their own story. Provide them with either Scaffold 1 or Scaffold 2 depending on their level of ability/experience. You can also provide them with a word bank to help them with their writing.

How to use the scaffolds

Scaffold 1

This scaffold is intended for younger/less experienced children. When cut out and assembled it makes a little storybook that the child can keep. It will take a little organising for the adult – but it is well worth it when the book is completed!

How to make the storybook:

1. Photocopy the required pages.
2. Cut around the page outlines.

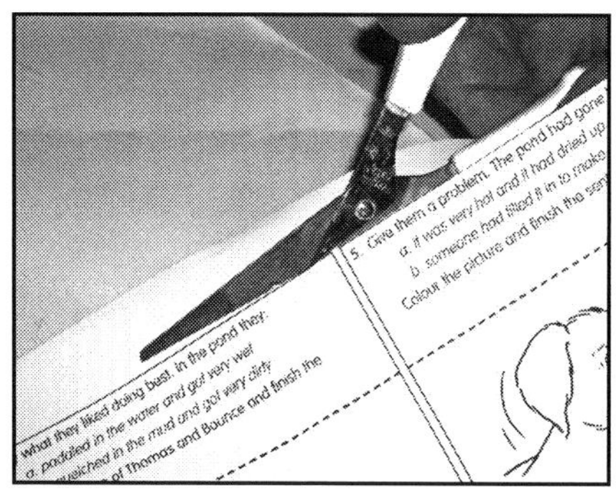

3. Glue the page with instructions 8 and 1 back to back with the page of instructions 2 and 7. (Or use a photocopier that prints on both sides.)

Do the same with the pages of instructions 6 and 3 and 4 and 5.

4. Fold the pages to make the book, ensuring the numbered instructions are in the correct order. Then sew or staple the pages in the centre (below the dotted line only).

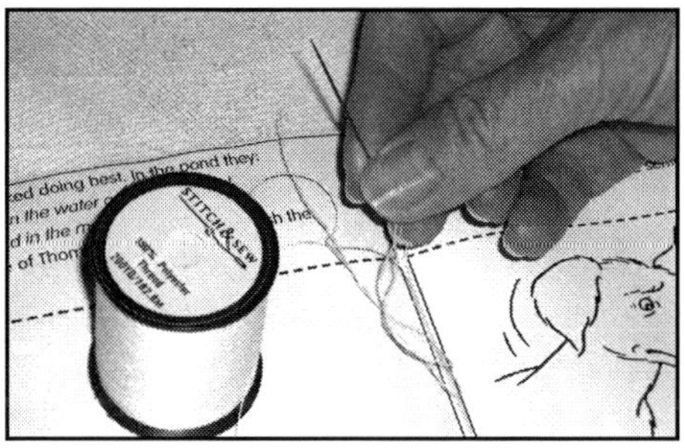

5. The book is now ready for the children to use. An adult can help them to read the instructions at the top of each page. The children draw and write the story. Note: the choices provided at the top of each page are guidelines only. The children may prefer to use their own ideas.

6. Once the book has been completed, the instructions should be cut off.

Scaffold 2

Scaffold 2 is intended for older or more able children. It provides them with suggestions for planning and then writing their own story. The children can select ideas from each section of the scaffold – 'The characters', 'The beginning', 'The middle' and 'The end' – or they can use their own ideas. This scaffold could also be used by children working in pairs or small groups. They could share ideas for each part of the story and then write their own.

Links to the National Literacy framework for Year 2

Unit 1 – Family life stories

Genre: Stories about familiar settings

Photocopiable activities:
page 8 – story sequencing
page 9 – exclamation marks (Term 1: S3)
page 10 – making lists/instructions (Term 1: T15, T16)

Unit 2 – Friendship stories

Genre: Stories about familiar settings

Photocopiable activities:
page 22 – story sequencing
page 23 – phrases that link sentences (Term 1: S2, T11)
page 24 – capital letters (Term 1: S5)

Unit 3 – Traditional fairy tales

Genre: Traditional stories and rhymes

Photocopiable activities:
page 36 – story sequencing
page 37 – antonyms (Term 2: W11)
page 38 – compound words (Term 2: W4)

Unit 4 – Indian tales

Genre: Stories from other cultures

Photocopiable activities:
page 50 – story sequencing
page 51 – character descriptions (Term 2: T14)
page 52 – speech marks (Term 2: S6)

Unit 5 – Humorous stories

Genre: Humorous stories

Photocopiable activities:
page 64 – story sequencing
page 65 – question words (Term 3: S6)
page 66 – synonyms (Term 3: W10)

Unit 6 – Adventure stories

Genre: Adventure stories

Photocopiable activities:
page 78 – story sequencing
page 79 – past tense of verbs (Term 3: S3)
page 80 – words linked to a topic (Term 3: W9)

Unit 1

Family life stories

Stories about family life are very popular. Children are immediately able to identify with the setting even if the family types and experiences don't quite match their own.

Family stories can be about all kinds of families and family situations:

- Siblings – *Titch* by Pat Hutchins – about being the smallest and youngest in the family;
- New family members – *Sophie and the New Baby* by Catherine and Laurence Anholt – about the changes that occur when a new baby arrives;
- Relationships – *Granpa* by John Burningham – about children sharing experiences with grandparents;
- Fears and worries – *Where's My Mum?* by Leon Rosselson – about a child's feelings of insecurity;
- Lifestyles – *Happy Families* series by Janet and Allan Ahlberg – about different occupations and family lifestyles;
- Biracial – *An African Princess* by Lyra Edmonds – about an Afro-American girl;
- Adoption – *We Wanted You* by Liz Rosenberg – about international adoption.

Family stories often have a dominant character in them, such as a very busy mother, an adventurous grandfather or an annoying sister. In such stories, the tale is usually told from the viewpoint of a member of the family who bears the brunt of these characters' behaviour. The writer does this to help the reader develop empathy with the character – most of us, after all, have similar people in our own families.

Apart from picture books intended to help children identify with themselves and their family situations, few family life stories are written exclusively about the everyday lives of the family – perhaps this would be too boring for the reader! Most family stories therefore also contain elements of other genres, such as mystery, adventure or fantasy.

Family stories usually have a happy ending.

Family life stories

Examples of family life stories

Love You Forever by Robert Munsch (Red Fox, 2001)

My Daddy is a Giant by Carl Norac (Macmillan Children's, 2004)

Just Like My Dad by David Melling (Hodder Children's, 2002)

My Big Brother, Boris by Liz Pichon (Scholastic, 2005)

You and Me, Little Bear by Martin Waddell (Walker Books, 2005)

Two Homes by Claire Masurel (Walker Books, 2002)

The Trouble with Mum by Babette Cole (Egmont Books, 2004)

Nutmeg Gets Adopted by Judith Foxon (British Association for Adoption and Fostering, 2001)

Granpa by John Burningham (Red Fox, 2003)

Humphrey's Family by Sally Hunter (Puffin, 2004)

A Present for Dad

by Roger Carr

Questions to ask and discussion ideas

Front cover
Read the title and the author's and illustrator's names. Ask the children to tell you what the story might be about. Who might the people be? Have they read other stories about birthdays? What happens on birthdays?

Pages 2 and 3
Why is Imran so excited? Where is his dad? What kind of work do you think his dad might do?

What does Imran want to do? What does his mother suggest?

Look at the picture. What can you see?

Pages 4 and 5
Where does Imran go to think about his dad's birthday gift? What is his back garden like? What does Imran decide to do?

Do you have a back garden? What is it like?

How difficult do you think it might be to plant a new lawn? What do you think Imran might have to do?

Pages 6 and 7
What do Imran and his mother decide to do? What is first on their list? What do you think they will use to dig out the weeds?

What is next on the list? Why do you think they need to dig the ground up?

What do they need to do after digging the ground? Why do you think they will need to do this?

Imran and his mum will need to buy seed and lawn food. Where might they go to get this?

What else do they need to do?

Do people in your family make lists? What sort of lists do they make? How does this help them?

Pages 8 and 9
Where did Imran go the next day? What did he ask the man behind the counter?

How long will the seed take to grow? How often will Imran need to water it?

When is Imran's dad coming home?

Who has been to a garden centre? What kinds of things can you buy there?

Page 10
What did Imran and his mother do every day after school? What did Imran use to dig the earth? What problem did he have? What did he feel like doing?

How did Imran's mum help him solve the problem?

Page 11
What did Imran's uncle use to dig the earth? How do you think this machine works?

What did Imran do after the digging? What is he going to do next?

Pages 12 and 13
What did Imran do after he had sown the seeds? What problem did Imran have? How did he solve this? What else could Imran do to get rid of the birds?

Pages 14 and 15
What did the grass look like when it first started to grow?

On what day did Imran's dad come home? What did Imran tell his father to do?

Page 16
What did Imran's dad say when he saw the new lawn? How happy do you think he felt? How do you think Imran was feeling?

Have you ever made something or done something special for someone's birthday? What did you do? How did the person feel? How did you feel? Has someone ever done something special for you? What did they do?

Name

Cut the pictures out.

Put them in order to tell the story of 'A Present for Dad'.

Name

Circle the exclamation marks (!).

?	.	!	?	!	.	.	!	?

Put an ! in each sentence below.

1. 'Mum ' Imran shouted.

2. 'I know what to give Dad for his birthday ' he called out.

3. 'Let's start, now ' said Imran.

4. 'It looks wonderful ' said his mum.

5. 'Happy birthday, Dad ' Imran shouted.

6. 'Oh wow ' said Imran's dad.

Finish each sentence. Use an exclamation mark.

1. 'Wow, that's ________________' said Tom.

2. 'Look out, don't _________________' shouted Sue.

3. 'Stop ____________________' shouted the policeman.

4. Katy yelled, 'Thanks __________________________'

5. 'Quick, let's hide in _____________________' said Andrew.

Name

Here are the instructions for planting a new lawn but they are in the wrong order. Rewrite them in the correct order.

1. Water the seeds.	1. ______________________
2. Buy the seeds.	2. ______________________
3. Rake the soil.	3. ______________________
4. Dig the ground.	4. ______________________
5. Sow the seeds.	5. ______________________

Make a list of all the things you would need to do to plan a birthday party.

Further activity ideas

Speaking and listening

- Talk about birthdays or other special events. What kinds of things do the children do on birthdays? What things do they usually eat? What games do they play? Do they give out invitations? Who organises the birthday party? What is the best birthday gift they have ever received? Why? Do they like going to birthday parties?

- Ask the children to mime the various stages of planting a new lawn (sowing, digging, weeding, raking, watering). Can the others guess what the actions are? Develop this into other areas of home life, such as housework, gardening or family outings.

- Set up a garden centre as a role play area. Make seed packets and bring in empty plastic bottles and pot plants. The children can take it in turns to be the customers and the shop assistant.

- Share ideas about the kinds of gifts we could give others without spending any money. Discuss the importance of giving and how good this can make us feel.

- Play memory games, such as 'I had a birthday party and I got a ...' where each child has to think up a new gift and the next child has to remember the list in order to pass on to the next child. You can make this more difficult by adding items in alphabetical order.

- Play party games that involve following instructions, such as 'Simon says' or a guided 'Pin the tail on the donkey' where the children work in pairs – one giving directions and the other being blindfolded.

Writing

- Design and make party invitations and cards. Discuss the various organisational features of each. You could create a real event, such as a class party where the children invite another class or their parents.

- Invent some party games. Ask the children to try them out in groups and then write out the instructions so other people can play them.

- Create memory books where each child makes a book about their past – 'When I was one I remember...' or 'Mum told me when I was one I...' The children could add drawings and photos. They could interview family members and add their anecdotes to the book.

- Ask the children to write about a recent birthday or other special occasion in their family. They could draw and label each family member to indicate the participants.

- Design birthday or special occasion cakes. Challenge the children to let their imaginations go wild! They can label and write a description of why their cake is so special.

- Create colourful balloons from paper. Ask the children to use dictionaries to find birthday or other special occasion words. They can write the words on the balloons as a word bank display.

- Where did Imran's dad work? Find out about places Imran's dad might have worked in (such as Spain, America or Australia). Write postcards from Imran's dad to Imran – include tourist information about these places. Use a world wall map to show where the places are. Pin the postcards to the map. The children could also 'write' back to him, inventing things they have been doing while he is away. You could also do this within UK countries only.

8. Finish the book blurb.

This story is about a family who had an uncle called Dan. Uncle Dan liked to invent things. One day he told the family that he wanted to

____

____

_______________________________________.

Read the story to find out what happened.

Unit 1 – Scaffold 1

1. Colour the picture.
   Write your name.

Uncle Dan

by ________________________________

2. You are going to write a story about a family who have an uncle called Dan. Choose who is in the family:
   a. Dad and Rick Smart
   b. Mum, Dad and Kim Brown

Draw the family next to Uncle Dan. Finish the sentences.

The ______________ family live at 24 Forest Drive. They have an uncle called __________ who lives in the house next door.

7. Say how the story ends. Uncle Dan decided to give up inventing things. He decided to:
   a. learn to play the trumpet instead
   b. breed noisy parrots instead

Draw Uncle Dan doing his new hobby and finish the sentence.

Uncle Dan decided to give up inventing things. Everyone was very pleased until he told them what he wanted to do instead. He had decided to ______________________________ ______________________________________.

6. Say what happened next. Uncle Dan was so pleased he gave them a treat. He:

   a. invited everyone over for a party

   b. took everyone out to the zoo

Draw the family enjoying their treat. Finish the sentence.

Uncle Dan was so happy he ______________

____

______________________________________.

3. Choose a good beginning. Uncle Dan was very strange. He:

   a. invented robots that always made a mess

   b. invented machines that always blew up

Draw Uncle Dan with one of his inventions and finish the sentence.

Uncle Dan was very strange. He __________

____

______________________________________.

4. Give the family a problem. One day Uncle Dan said he was lonely and that he wanted to:

   a. sell his house and move in with them

   b. visit them every day with one of his inventions

   Draw Uncle Dan looking sad. Finish the sentence.

One day Uncle Dan visited the family. He looked very sad. He said he was lonely and he wanted to ______________________________

______________________________.

The family were very worried.

5. Say what the family did. They didn't want to hurt Uncle Dan's feelings so they:

   a. bought him a dog to keep him company

   b. told him they would visit him every day

   Colour the picture and finish the sentence.

The family liked Uncle Dan but they did not want his inventions! So to stop him feeling lonely they ______________________________

______________________________.

Uncle Dan
Word bank

bought	instead	parrots
company	invent	robots
decided	inventing	strange
everyone	invention	treat
family	invited	trumpet
feelings	liked	uncle
happy	lonely	very
house	machines	visit
hurt	noisy	worried

My own words

Aunty's Birthday Party
by _____________________

You are going to plan and write a story about a family.
Use the information below to help you or use your own ideas.

The characters

Choose the characters for your story.

a) Mum, Dad and their son, Simon

or

b) Mum and daughter, Melanie

The family are planning a special surprise birthday party for their aunty.

Give their aunty a name. ______________________________

How old will she be on her birthday?______________

The beginning

How will your story begin?

a) The family are sitting in the kitchen. They are making a list of things to do for the party. They decide who is going to do what. Mum decides that she is going to bake a cake.

or

b) The family are in the garden. It is a warm, sunny day. They are planning the party for Aunty. Mum decides to make it fancy dress. She wants to dress up in a clown's costume.

What do the other people in the family want to do?

____

The middle

What happens?

The day of the party arrives. Everything looks really good. Aunty is very happy at the party. But then something happens:

a) *The dogs from next door run into the room. They knock all the food over and eat Aunty's cake.*

or

b) *The party is so noisy that all the neighbours knock on the door. They are not very happy.*

What does Mum do?____

The end

What happens in the end?

Aunty is so pleased with the party that she decides:

a) *She wants an even bigger party next year.*

or

b) *She is going to have a birthday every month instead of just once a year!*

How do the family feel about this? What do they do?

____

____

Aunty's Birthday Party
Word bank

balloons	escape	knock
bigger	everyone	neighbours
birthday	everything	next
complain	family	party
costume	fancy dress	people
daughter	garden	planning
decided	happy	surprise
decision	invites	telephone
enjoying	kitchen	upset

My own words

Unit 2

Friendship stories

Stories about friendships are very important for children of all ages. They can offer powerful lessons about sharing, appreciating differences and getting on with others. Through the safe medium of a fictional character, the reader can explore their own problems and issues associated with growing up and maintaining friendships. These characters need not be human; many friendship stories are about animals. Perhaps it is easier to empathise with a cute animal character than a very real human one!

Friendship stories can address particular issues such as:

- breaking up and making friends again (for example, *You're Not My Best Friend Anymore* by Charlotte Pomerantz);
- making new friends (for example, *Elmer's New Friend* by David McKee);
- friendships with pets (for example, *I'll Always Love You* by Hans Wilhelm);
- sticking up for or looking after your friends (for example, *Best of Friends!* by Shen Roddie and Sally Anne Lambert).

Some authors have written books specifically about friendship but most genres contain aspects of friendships between the characters, whether it be a fantasy, science fiction or adventure story.

Friendship stories

Examples of friendship stories

My Friend Bear by Jez Alborough (Walker Books, 2004)

Elmer's New Friend by David McKee (Andersen Press Ltd, 2002)

Little Polar Bear Finds a Friend by Hans de Beer (North-South Books, 1996)

Friends by Kathryn Care (Hodder Children's, 2004)

On a Tall, Tall Cliff by Andrew Murray (HarperCollins, 2004)

Fox Makes Friends by Adam Relf (Macmillan, 2005)

Old Bear and His Friends by Jane Hissey (Red Fox, 1991)

What Friends Do Best by Jonathan Emmett (HarperCollins, 2005)

Friends by Kim Lewis (Walker Books, 1999)

What Are Friends For? by Sally Grindley (Kingfisher, 2000)

Elmer's Friends by David McKee (Milet Publishing, 1998)

My Best Friends by Anna Nilsen (Zero to Ten, 2005)

Johann and the Birds

by Sarah Prince

Questions to ask and discussion ideas

Front cover
Read the title and the author's and illustrator's names. Ask the children to tell you what the story might be about. What kind of person do they think Johann might be? Which country might he live in? What sorts of things might he do? Why do they think the birds like him? What kind of birds are they?

Pages 2 and 3
What kind of pets did Johann have? Why do you think he liked them so much? What names do you think he might have called them? Where did the birds live?

What did Johann do early every morning? What did the pigeons do? Why do you think he let them fly out of their cages? What do you think the birds will do next?

Pages 4 and 5
What did the pigeons do after Johann let them out? What would Johann do? Where do you think the pigeons went?

Why do you think the pigeons always returned to Johann every night?

Look at the picture. What can you see? Where is Johann's house? Where do you think he lives – in the country or the city? What kind of house does he live in?

Pages 6 and 7
What happened to Johann one day? What was wrong with him? Where were the birds? Who came to visit Johann? What did he want Johann to do? What do you think might happen to the birds?

Pages 8 and 9
What did the doctor tell Johann? Why was Johann upset? What did he tell Mr Edgar to do? Why do you think he asked him to do this?

What can you see in the picture? Have you been to a hospital? What was it like?

What do you think might happen next?

Pages 10 and 11
What did Mr Edgar do? What did the birds do?

What happened when Mr Edgar returned to lock up the birds for the night? Why do you think they did not come back? What do you think may have happened to the birds?

Pages 12 and 13
What does Mr Edgar do next? How does he get there? Why is Mr Edgar so worried?

Do you think Mr Edgar is a good friend to Johann? Why?

What do you think Johann is going to say when Mr Edgar tells him about the birds?

Pages 14 and 15
What did Mr Edgar see when he opened the door? How do you think Mr Edgar was feeling? How do you think Johann was feeling? How do you think the nurses and doctor might be feeling?

Page 16
What do you think this means?

> 'My heart may not be strong but it's big enough to love all my friends.'

How many friends do you have? Can you care about more than one friend? Do you think animals can be friends to you as well as people?

How can people show they are your friend? How can animals show they are your friend?

How can you be a good friend to others? How can you be a friend to an animal?

Name

Cut the pictures out.

Put them in order to tell the story of 'Johann and the Birds'.

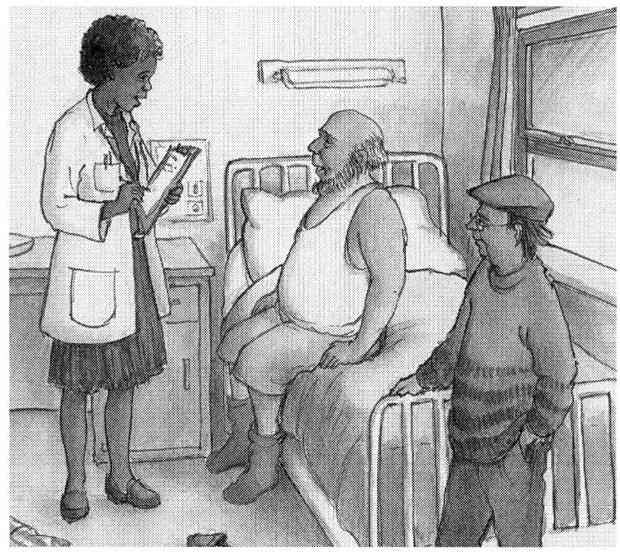

Name

Choose words from the box to start the sentences.

suddenly	one day	every morning	then
as soon as	later that day	once there was	

1. ______________________________ an old man named Johann.

2. __________________________ Johann was up bright and early.

3. ___________________________ he opened the cages, the birds would fly high into the sky.

4. ________________ they would fly off for their day's adventure.

5. __________________________________ Johann would wait for them to return.

6. _________________________ Johann was not well.

7. ____________________ Johann remembered his birds.

Finish these sentences using your own ideas.

1. After a while ____

2. Suddenly ____

3. When he had finished ______________________________________

4. Then ____

5. Meanwhile ____

Name

Rewrite these sentences, putting in all the capital letters.

1. 'johann and the birds' was written by sarah prince.

____

2. johann's friend was called mr edgar.

____

3. mr edgar took johann to the hospital.

____

Invent 10 names for Johann's birds.

1. ________________
2. ________________
3. ________________
4. ________________
5. ________________
6. ________________
7. ________________
8. ________________
9. ________________
10. ________________

Invent an address for Johann.
Write it here.

____
____
____
____
____
____

Further activity ideas

Speaking and listening

- Ask the children to tell you about their pets. What kinds of animals do they have? How do they care for them? You could invite a member of the RSPCA to talk to the children about caring for animals.
- Talk about how Mr Edgar cared for Johann by visiting him and making sure he was all right. Share ideas about how we can help others. How can the chldren help their parents? Neighbours? School friends?
- Invite someone in to talk about the hobby of racing pigeons. Ask the children to each prepare a question before the visit for a question and answer session.
- How well do the children recognise each other's voices? Play 'Your friend'. Ask one child to sit in a chair with his back to the rest of the class. Select a child from the audience by pointing or tapping the child's shoulder (so the child in the chair cannot see who it is). The selected child says 'Hello.' The child in the chair says 'Who's there?' The other child says 'Your friend.' The child in the chair has to guess who it is by the voice alone. If they guess correctly the other child sits in the seat. If not, they have another turn with a new child. If this becomes too easy, the children can try funny voices!
- Set up some related role play situations, such as a hospital ward or a pet shop.

Writing

- Ask the children to draw a picture of their best friend. They could then write words or sentences to say why they like this person/what is special about this person.
- The children could write a book about their friends, called 'Me and My Friends', where they draw and write about each friend on a different page; for example, 'My friend Alex and I play football,' and 'I like my friend Max because he helps me with my spelling.'
- Remind the children that Johann had names for each of his 100 pigeons! Make an ABC of names – can they think up 100?
- Bring in a collection of get well cards. Discuss the kinds of things that are on the front and the messages inside. The children could make a get well card for Johann or someone they know who is unwell.
- Find out about how to care for birds. Make a class book about birds and how to care for them. Groups of children could be responsible for different sections of the book; for example, 'Some birds found in the UK', 'How to care for wild birds', 'How to care for caged birds', 'All about pigeons' and so on.
- The children could read and write stories about people and their pets.
- Ask the children to imagine what Johann's birds got up to when they flew away for the day. Where did they go? What things did they see? What adventures did they have? They could write 'The pigeons' story'!
- Invent a life for Mr Edgar. What hobbies did he have? What things did he do with Johann? Where did he live? What was his family like? Did he have any pets? The children could draw Mr Edgar and write some sentences about him.
- Tell the children how pigeons have been used to carry messages. Invite them to send a message to someone in their family or a storybook character via pigeon post! They could write them on paper that is rolled into something suitable, such as a plastic film cartridge.

8. Finish the book blurb.

This story is about two friends called Naseem and Jake. They always played together. One day ______________________

____

______________________________.

Read the story to find out what happened.

Unit 2 – Scaffold 1

1. Colour the picture.
   Write your name.

Naseem and Jake

by ______________________________

2. You are going to write a story about two friends called Naseem and Jake. Choose where they both lived:
   a. in houses with gardens
   b. in a block of flats

   Draw Naseem's and Jake's homes. Finish the sentence.

Naseem and Jake were best friends. They both lived in a ______________________ ______________________ in George Street.

7. Say how the story ends. Naseem was so happy he:
   a. gave Jake his best football card
   b. asked him to stay for tea

   Colour the picture and finish the sentence.

Naseem and Jake became friends again. Naseem was so happy his bike was fixed he ______________________________ ______________________________.

6. Say how the problem was solved. Jake:
   a. asked Naseem's dad to help him fix the bike
   b. told Naseem he was sorry and helped him fix the bike

   Draw Jake fixing the bike. Finish the sentence.

Jake listened to what his ______________ said and he __________________________________

____.

3. Choose a good beginning. Naseem and Jake liked to:
   a. play football together
   b. play in the park together

   Draw Naseem and Jake. Finish the sentence.

Naseem and Jake played together every day. They liked to ______________________________

____.

4. Give the friends a problem. One day Jake broke Naseem's bike. Naseem did not want to be friends any more. He:

   a. stopped walking to school with Jake

   b. did not come to see Jake

   Colour the picture. Finish the sentence.

One day Jake broke Naseem's bike. He did not mean to do it. Naseem did not want to be friends with Jake any more. He ________ ______________________________.

5. Say what happened next. Jake:

   a. asked his mum what to do

   b. asked his teacher what to do

   Colour the picture. Finish the sentence.

Jake was very sad. He wanted Naseem to be his friend again so he asked ____________ ______________________________.

Naseem and Jake
Word bank

again	friends	park
any	garden	played
asked	happy	sad
bike	helped	sorry
broke	house	teacher
fix	liked	together
fixed	listened	unhappy
flat	lived	very
football	mum	

My own words

Best friends

by ____________________

You are going to plan and write a story about two friends.
Use the information below to help you or use your own ideas.

The characters

Choose the characters for your story.

a) Simone and Lucy

or

b) Michael and Paul

The friends like doing the same hobby/sport.

What is this hobby/sport?______________________________

Where do they live?______________________________________

The beginning

How will your story begin?

a) The two friends are walking home from school. They are planning what to do before tea. They begin to fight over what they want to do.

or

b) The two friends are playing in the park. One of them wants to stay longer but the other one wants to go home. They begin to fight with each other.

How do they feel when they are fighting?

____

The middle

What happens?

There is a tree near the two friends. One of them suddenly sees:

a) a cat stuck on one of the branches. It is crying to get down.

or

b) John, a boy from their school, stuck in the tree. He is calling out for them to help him.

What do they decide to do?

____

____

____

The end

What happens in the end?

The two friends feel very pleased that they were able to help. It makes them forget they had been fighting. They decide to:

a) have a party.
or
b) write to the newspaper about what happened.

What did the cat do?

____

or

What did John do?

____

Best Friends
Word bank

best	frightened	pleased
calling	happy	rescue
climbed	help	safely
crying	helpful	scared
decided	ladder	scratched
fight	newspaper	stuck
fighting	party	suddenly
fire brigade	planning	very
friends	playing	worried

My own words

Unit 3

Traditional fairy tales

Fairy tales are magical morality tales where the 'good' characters triumph over evil and restore order. These traditional stories usually have a range of stock characters: a weak father, a wicked stepmother, a heroine who is as good as she is beautiful, a handsome prince, a wicked witch, a dutiful youngest son and a magical animal or creature who helps the hero or heroine. The heroine of the story is essentially rather passive, but she can be spurred into action by dire need or when given a helping hand by a magical character. Although the hero or heroine is usually given a name, many of the characters are known simply by their position in society or their relationship to the protagonist; for example, 'the king' and 'Jack's mother'.

Weak characters may come to realise the error of their ways by the end of the tale, but wicked characters rarely change and frequently meet their end in particularly gruesome ways. The plot often includes a contrast between the ways a good character and a wicked character respond to a challenge or adversity.

The setting for fairy tales is beautiful countryside dotted with wonderful castles. The forests in this countryside are home to wild beasts, which often help the hero or heroine.

As well as using character types, writers of traditional fairy tales use antiquated language and conventional phrases, such as:

Once upon a time...
...as good as she was beautiful...
He set off to make his fortune.
They lived happily ever after.

Conventional similes or similes drawn from the natural world are another feature of these stories:

Her skin was as white as snow.

Some of the characters speak in rhyme:

Mirror, mirror, on the wall
Who is the fairest of them all?

Fairy tales are usually narrated in the third person, sometimes in a wry tone, and may contain repetition of certain phrases.

Traditional fairy tales

Examples of traditional fairy tales

A First Book of Fairy Tales retold by Mary Hoffman (Dorling Kindersley, 2001)

The Usborne Book of Fairy Tales retold by Heather Amery (Usborne, 2004)

The Oxford Treasury of Fairy Tales by Geraldine McCaughrean (Oxford University Press, 2003)

The Fairy Tales by Jan Pieñkowski (Puffin, 2005)

The Complete Illustrated Stories of Hans Christian Andersen (Bounty Books, 2001)

The Hutchinson Treasury of Fairy Tales (Hutchinson Children's, 1999)

Jack and the Beanstalk by Richard Walker (Barefoot Books, 2000)

The Ugly Duckling by Ian Beck (Orchard Books, 1999)

The Elves and the Shoemaker

by Meg Stein

Questions to ask and discussion ideas

Front cover
Read the title and the author's and illustrator's names. Ask the children to tell you if they have heard this story before. What might it be about? What are elves? What do they know about them?

Do they think the story is about people today or in the past? Why do they think this?

Pages 2 and 3
Why do you think the people were poor? What did they do all day? What did the shoemaker use to make the shoes? Why do you think they look so sad?

What did they do with their last bit of leather? Where did they leave it?

What do you think might happen?

Page 4
What did the shoemaker and his wife find the next morning? How do you think they felt? Who do you think made the shoes? Why do you think they did this?

Look at the picture. What can you see? What do the shoes look like?

Page 5
Who comes into the shop? Do you think they are rich or poor? What tells you this? What kind of clothes are they wearing?

What does the man do? What does he say?

Pages 6 and 7
What did the shoemaker and his wife do with the money? Why do you think they were so pleased?

How many pairs of shoes did they cut out of the leather?

What did they find in the morning? What were the shoes like? Who do you think made them? Who do you think will buy them?

Pages 8 and 9
What happened that day? Who bought the shoes? Who did he buy them for?

How much leather could the shoemaker buy now?

Look at the picture. What can you see?

Pages 10 and 11
What happened over the next days? How do you think it made the shoemaker and his wife feel? How do you think it changed their lives?

Look at the picture. What changes can you see in the shoemaker and his wife?

What did they decide to do one night? What do you think they will see?

Pages 12 and 13
What did the shoemaker and his wife see? What were they doing? What kind of shoe are they making in the picture?

What do the elves look like? What are their clothes like? What size are they?

What did the shoemaker's wife say they should do for the elves? Do you think they will be pleased? Why?

Pages 14 and 15
What did the elves do when they saw the clothes? Why do you think they danced around the room? What were the clothes like? Which outfit do you like best? Why?

Page 16
What do you think happened to the elves after they left the shoemaker and his wife?

Why do you think the elves helped the shoemaker in the first place?

What did you like best about this story?

Name

Cut the pictures out.

Put them in order to tell the story of 'The Elves and the Shoemaker'.

Name

Match the opposites.
One has been done for you.

unhappy	poor
night	small
rich	happy
first	old
hard	hot
new	last
big	soft
cold	day

Use five of these words in sentences.

1. ______________________________

2. ______________________________

3. ______________________________

4. ______________________________

5. ______________________________

Name

Join words to make new words.
Write them underneath. You can use each word more than once. One has been done for you.

butter	end
week	day
out	thing
to	light
some	fly
moon	ball
foot	side

butterfly ____________ ____________

____________ ____________ ____________

____________ ____________ ____________

Use two of your new words in sentences.

1. ____

2. ____

Further activity ideas

Speaking and listening

- Use the story to begin a discussion about shoes. What are the shoes like in the story? Would the children wear these shoes today? How many different pairs of shoes do they have? Do they have shoes for different purposes – such as for dancing, sport, being at home, walking the dog, hiking and so on? What is special about them? Why do they need to be different? Which shoes are their favourites? Why? What makes a shoe comfortable?
- Set up a shoe shop as a role play area. The children could take turns in making, selling and buying the shoes.
- Invent a story surrounding the owner of the first shoe the shoemaker made. This could be done with the children sitting in a circle. You could begin: 'Once there lived a man and his wife. They were very rich. Their names were...' The first child could decide what they were called. You could then continue building up the story with the children making the suggestions. They could decide: where they lived, who the shoe was for, why they wanted the shoe so much, what happened to the person who wore the shoe – was it magic?
- Ask the children to bring in from home/choose from the library their favourite fairy tale. Ask them to share the book with a friend – to show them their favourite pictures and to say why they like the story.
- Share other stories about shoes, such as 'Cinderella'.
- Talk about stories where some of the characters are fairies, elves, dwarfs or other non-human and usually magical beings (Tinkerbell in 'Peter Pan', the dwarfs in 'Snow White', the beast in 'Beauty and the Beast'). Can the children suggest any other stories in which they appear? Why do they think people use such characters? Do people enjoy reading about them?

Writing

- Ask the children to design a shoe or boot. They could draw and colour it, then label all its special features. They could also design and make an advertisement to sell it.
- Bring in some old catalogues and ask the children to select and cut out pictures of shoes they like. They could select them according to categories, such as sports shoes, school shoes and slippers. Each child could write why they like the shoe they have chosen.
- Look at different types of shoe fastenings. Share ideas about how they work and which ones they think are best. The children could write instructions for using the fastenings correctly; for example, 'How to tie shoelaces'.
- Ask the children to write the story from the elves' point of view. Why did they help the shoemaker and his wife? What did they think of their new clothes? Where did they go in the end? Did they go off and help someone else?
- The shoemaker was fortunate to have the elves help him overcome his poverty. Find out about charities that help the poor and needy today. Make a class book about people who help others. The children could contact one of the charities and raise money for their appeal.
- Ask the children to make a poster of as many non-human characters from stories as they can think of and label them.
- Ask the children to choose their favourite non-human character and write a new short illustrated story for that character.

8. Finish the book blurb.

This story is about a princess who had a spell put on her. This made her very sad. One day

____

______________________________________.

Read the story to find out what happened.

Unit 3 – Scaffold 1

1. Colour the picture.
Write your name.

The Sad Princess

by ______________________________

2. You are going to write a fairy tale about a princess who was always sad. Choose where she lived:

   a. in a big palace made from gold

   b. in a castle with a hundred towers

   Draw where the princess lived. Finish the sentence.

Once upon a time there lived a princess who was always sad. She lived with her parents, the king and queen, in a ______________________

______________________________________.

7. Say how the story ends. The prince and princess:

   a. got married

   b. became very best friends

   Colour the picture and finish the sentence.

Everyone in the kingdom was very happy. The prince and princess ______________________

______________________________________.

And everyone lived happily ever after.

6. Say how the problem was solved. The prince:
   a. captured and killed the witch
   b. climbed the tower and passed a magic potion through the princess's window

Colour the picture. Finish the sentence.

The prince ______________________________
______________________________.
The spell was broken! The princess was happy again!

3. Choose a good beginning. The princess was always sad because a witch had put a spell on her. She would turn into a mouse if she:
   a. went outside
   b. had any visitors

Colour the picture and finish the sentences.

The princess was always sad because a witch had ______________________. The spell would turn her into a ______________ if she ______________________.

4. The king and queen wanted someone to get rid of the spell so they offered a reward of:
   a. a bag of gold
   b. a chest of jewels

Colour the picture. Finish the sentence.

The king and queen wanted to help the princess so they offered a big reward of

____________________________________.

5. Say what happened next. A prince came to see the king and queen. He said he could help the princess. He was:
   a. brave and very handsome
   b. kind and caring

Draw the prince. Finish the sentence.

One day a prince came to see the king and queen. He said he could help the princess. The prince was________________________

____________________________________.

The Sad Princess
Word bank

after
brave
broken
captured
caring
castle
climbed
everyone
friends
handsome
happily
happy
hundred
jewels
kind
king
kingdom
magic
married
palace
potion
prince
princess
problem
queen
reward
spell
tower
witch

My own words

The Brave Prince
by ____________________

You are going to plan and write a fairy tale.
Use the information below to help you or use your own ideas.

The characters

Choose the characters for your story.

a) A king and queen and their beautiful daughter, the princess

or

b) A poor washerwoman and her lovely daughter

Where do the characters live?

____

The story also has a wicked witch in it.

Where does the witch live?______________________________

The beginning

How will your story begin?

a) The witch tricks the daughter into visiting her. She locks her in a cage.

or

b) The witch dresses up as a flower seller and visits the daughter. She puts a spell on her. The spell puts her to sleep.

Why does the witch do this?

____

How do the daughter's family feel?

____

The middle

What happens?

The family meet a stranger who is dressed in rags. He says he can help them. The stranger is really a handsome prince.

The stranger:

a) gets all the creatures in the forest to help him

or

b) thinks of a clever way of tricking the witch to let the girl go or break the spell.

What do the creatures do? or How does he trick the witch?

____

____

____

The end

What happens in the end?

The prince saves the daughter. Everyone is very happy.

a) The prince marries the daughter.

or

b) The prince stays in the kingdom forever to look after everyone.

What happens to the witch?

____

And they all lived happily ever after.

The Brave Prince
Word bank

after	family	potion
asleep	forest	queen
awakes	handsome	saves
beautiful	happily	spell
brave	kind	stranger
clever	king	tricks
creatures	lovely	unlocks
daughter	magic	washerwoman
everyone	poor	wicked witch

My own words

Indian tales

Traditional Indian tales are largely based on folk tales, myths and legends that are part of the oral tradition. Because most of these stories were created before many people could read or write, they were passed on from generation to generation by word of mouth. Each storyteller would place emphasis on the parts of the story he or she felt were the most important for delivering the message. Consequently, no two storytellers would tell the story in the same way.

Indian tales are usually concerned with the power of faith and the victory of good over evil. Often, reflecting Indian society, the main character will be poor and will have to struggle to survive, overcoming both practical and supernatural difficulties. There are usually both material and moral rewards to be gained, such as wealth, fine clothing, jewellery and a rich lifestyle, happiness and contentment.

There are often references to the climate, landscape, animals and the jobs people do, such as farming, fishing or selling crafts and produce at markets. Because of the intense heat, the threat of drought and famine are common themes in many Indian stories.

Another aspect of Indian storytelling is that of deities, spirits and the supernatural. In addition, the Hindu faith has many gods and goddesses who appear in stories as powerful forces. Usually, a measure of sacrifice on the part of the main character is required in order to pass a 'test' before being rewarded.

Indian tales

Examples of Indian tales

Jamil's Clever Cat: A Bengali Folk Tale by Fiona French (Frances Lincoln, 2000)

Tales from Around the World (Zero to Ten, 2005)

Rama and the Demon King: A Tale of Ancient India by Jessica Souhami (Frances Lincoln, 1998)

Magical Stories from India by Pratima Mitchell (Longman, 2001)

www.indolink.com/Kidz/mythology.html

www.indianchild.com

The Ungrateful Tiger

by Julie Ellis

Questions to ask and discussion ideas

Front cover
Read the title and the author's and illustrator's names. Explain the meaning of the word 'ungrateful'.

Ask the children to tell you what they already know about tigers. In which country do they live in the wild? Show them India on a map. What do they already know about India? Do they know anyone who has lived there?

What might happen in the story?

Pages 2 and 3
What is the boy's name? Where does he live? What kind of place is it? What do the houses look like? What might they be made from?

What is a jungle? What kinds of things might be found there?

Why were the villagers frightened? What did they decide to do? What do you think might happen next?

What kinds of clothing are the people wearing? What have they got on their heads?

Pages 4 and 5
What chore was Sunni doing that morning? How was he carrying the firewood? What do you think he was going to do with it?

What sound did Sunni hear? What did he find? What did the tiger ask Sunni to do? Do you think he will help him? What would you do if you came across a tiger in a pit?

Pages 6 and 7
How did Sunni feel when he saw the tiger in the pit? Why do you think he felt like this? What did Sunni say to the tiger? What did the tiger say back?

What did Sunni do in the end? How did the tiger get out?

What do you think will happen next?

Pages 8 and 9
Why was Sunni scared when the tiger got out of the pit? What did he say to the tiger? What did the tiger say to Sunni? Do you think this was fair? Why do you think the tiger went back on his word?

How do you think Sunni is feeling now? What do you think might happen?

Pages 10 and 11
Who came along to help Sunni? What did the elephant say? Why do you think Sunni agreed so quickly?

What is the elephant wearing? Why do you think he has these things on?

Where else in the world do elephants live? Do you know the differences between an Indian and an African elephant?

Pages 12 and 13
What did the elephant suggest the tiger should do? What did the elephant do?

Why do you think the elephant asked the tiger to do this? What do you think will happen next?

Pages 14 and 15
Why was the elephant so clever? How do you think Sunni is feeling now? How do you think the tiger is feeling?

Do you think the elephant was right to do what he did?

Page 16
What do you think will happen to the tiger now?

What did you like about the story?

Name

Cut out the pictures.

Put them in order to tell the story of 'The Ungrateful Tiger'.

Name

Choose words from the box to describe the tiger in the story. Circle the words.

small	big
unfair	fair
grateful	ungrateful
brave	scared
strong	weak
kind	mean
old	young
happy	unhappy
clever	silly
bad	good

Draw Sunni in one box. Write some words to describe him in the other.

Name

Circle the speech marks in each sentence.
The first one has been done for you.

1. ' What is making that noise? ' he wondered.

2. When the tiger saw Sunni it cried, ' Help! '

3. ' Wait! ' said the tiger.

4. ' That's not fair, ' cried Sunni. ' You tricked me. '

5. ' Show me where you were when Sunni found you, ' said the elephant to the tiger.

Rewrite these sentences, writing in the speech marks.
The first one has been done for you.

1. I like elephants, said Sunni.
   'I like elephants,' said Sunni.

2. You tricked me, said the tiger.

   ____

3. You tricked me too, said Sunni.

   ____

4. I think the tiger has learned his lesson, said the elephant.

   ____

Further activity ideas

Speaking and listening

- Use the story to begin a discussion about being fair to others. When do the children think people are being unfair to them at home? At school? Are they always fair to others? Has anyone ever told them they are ungrateful? How has this made them feel? What kinds of things should we be grateful for (such as clean water, our family, our home)?

- Listen to some Indian music, perhaps with a sitar playing. How does the music make them feel? How different is it from the music they like to listen to at home?

- If possible, invite a person who has lived in India to speak to the class. The children could prepare a question each to ask the visitor. The visitor could talk about what it is like to live there – the climate, the buildings, clothing, houses, food and countryside. How does it differ from life in the UK?

- Read and share other traditional tales from India – what else can the children learn about Indian culture from reading the stories?

- Explore questions. Ask the children to think up five questions they would like to ask Sunni, five questions to ask the tiger and five questions to ask the elephant. The questions need not be about the story – they could be about the 'real' life of each character. Can the children suggest possible answers?

- Use the story to discuss being brave and feeling scared. Was Sunni brave to let the tiger out? How do they think he felt when the tiger said he was going to eat him? Talk about how everyone is afraid of something. What things are the children afraid of? (Such as the dark.) How can they overcome some of these fears? When have the children felt brave? Who do they think are brave people (such as the police or soldiers)?

Writing

- Find out about tigers. Where do they live? What do they eat? What is special about them? The children could use internet sites and information books to help them find information. They could create a fact file about tigers.

- The children could make information books about India. They could work in groups with each group contributing a different section to the book, such as climate, houses, animals and food.

- What do the children already know about elephants? Ask them to write down their ideas. They could then find out more about them – especially Indian elephants. They could then write 'New things I have learned about elephants'.

- Draw a template outline of a tiger and/or elephant and photocopy them. The children could use a dictionary to find suitable words to describe the animal and write their words inside the shape for display.

- More able children could use the words describing the tiger or elephant to make acrostic poems:

  t errifying
  i ndia
  g rowling
  e scape
  r are

- Who else does the elephant help? The children could write another story on a day in the life of the elephant.

- Discuss how the Indian elephant and tiger are both animals that need our protection. Find out how we can help endangered/at risk animals and plants. Encourage the children to explore sites such as www.worldwildlife.org, www.greenpeace.org, www.foe.org and www.adoptwildlife.org. They could create a list of things we can do to help animals and plants – in the school grounds, at home, in the UK and in the world.

8. Finish the book blurb.

This story is a folk tale from India. It is about the time when elephants could fly! The people got fed up with ____________________

____

____.

Read the story to find out what happened.

Unit 4 – Scaffold 1

1. Colour the picture.
   Write your name.

When Elephants Could Fly

a story adapted from a folk tale from Orissa

by ____________________

2. You are going to write a tale set in India. It is about the time when elephants could fly. Choose how to begin:

    a. Once, very long, long ago

    b. There once was a time when

Colour the picture and finish the sentence.

____

______________ elephants could fly! God rode on an elephant when he made the world.

7. Say how the story ends. The elephants ran away into the forest. They were:

    a. very sad

    b. glad they didn't break any more houses

Colour the picture and finish the sentence.

When the elephants woke up and saw their wings had gone they ____________________

____

______________________________________.

6. Say what happened. God cut off their wings. He gave two to the peacock and two to the banana plant. The people were very happy. They:
   a. had their own big feast
   b. started to fix their broken houses

   Draw the happy people. Finish the sentence.

God cut off the elephants' wings. He gave two to the peacock and two to the banana plant. The people were so happy they

____

______________________________.

3. Say what the elephants were like. The elephants were very happy and would:
   a. sometimes sing like birds
   b. chase each other through the sky

   Draw the elephants and finish the sentence.

The elephants were very happy and they would ______________________________

______________________________.

4. Give the story a problem. The elephants sat on the roofs of houses but they were so heavy they broke the houses. The people:

a. were very upset

b. tried to keep the elephants away

Colour the picture. Finish the sentence.

The elephants liked to sit on the roofs of houses. They were so heavy they broke the houses. The people ______________________

______________________________________.

5. Say how the problem was solved. God invited all the animals to a feast. The elephants ate so much they:

a. fell asleep under the trees

b. fell asleep near the river

Draw the elephants asleep. Finish the sentence.

One day God decided to help the people. He invited all the animals to a big feast. The elephants ate so much they______________

______________________________________.

When Elephants Could Fly
Word bank

animals
asleep
banana
birds
break
broke
chase
elephant
feast
forest
happy
heavy
houses
India
once
peacock
people
roofs
sad
sing
unhappy
upset
wings
woke

My own words

Simret and the Snake
by ____________________

You are going to plan and write a tale set in India.
Use the information below to help you or use your own ideas.

The characters

Choose the characters for your story.

a) A poor farmer, his wife and their daughter Simret

or

b) A poor fisherman and his daughter Simret

What kind of village do the characters live in?

____

What is their house like? ____

The beginning

How will your story begin?

a) One day Simret goes out to collect firewood for the family's cooking fire.

or

b) One day Simret goes to visit her sick aunt in the next village.

On the way Simret comes across a snake who wants her to carry him across the river where there are more things to eat.

What does the snake say he will do if Simret does not help him?

____

The middle

What happens?

Simret is very brave and agrees to help the snake.
She:

a) ties some string around him and helps pull him through the water.

or

b) gently holds the snake in her arms and they start to wade across together.

Halfway across Simret lets the snake go, showing him how to swim. The snake is very pleased and reaches the other side safely.

The end

What happens in the end?

The snake was so grateful to Simret that he:

a) asked all the animals of the forest to gather food for Simret's village so that no-one ever went hungry again.

or

b) showed Simret where some treasure was hidden and she and her family were never poor again.

What did Simret do?

____

From that day on snakes have always been able to swim and Simret's family were always happy.

Simret and the Snake
Word bank

again	house	swimming
animals	hungry	together
collect	India	treasure
daughter	pleased	village
firewood	poor	visit
forest	river	wade
gather	safely	water
helpful	snake	
hidden	swim	

My own words

Unit 5

Humorous stories

Writing a story intended to make someone laugh and to entertain them is a challenge. After all, every reader has a slightly different sense of humour. Authors of comic stories sometimes employ a first person narrator and adopt an informal, conspiratorial tone. It is through the eyes of this stock hero that events unfold.

The characters of humorous stories often have amusing or alliterative names and appear slightly larger than life. The 'good' characters triumph at the conclusion of the tale. Animal characters are another common feature of humorous stories.

Amusing stories often contain an element of slapstick – knockabout or rough-and-tumble humour. This may take the form of a series of disasters but, as in the best cartoons, the characters pick themselves up and dust themselves down after even the most horrible of experiences.

Comic stories may include puns, jokes and hyperbole, which is deliberate exaggeration used for effect.

Humorous stories

Examples of humorous stories

A Pipkin of Pepper by Helen Cooper (Picture Corgi, 2005)

The Tale of Jack Frost by David Melling (Barron's Educational, 2003)

Funny Stories for 7 Year Olds chosen by Helen Paiba (Macmillan, 1998)

Scared of a Bear by Hilda Offen (Hodder Children's, 1996)

Five Minutes' Peace by Jill Murphy (Walker Books, 2001)

Yuck! by Mick Manning (Frances Lincoln, 2005)

I Don't Want to Go to Bed by Tony Ross (HarperCollins, 2005)

Little Rabbit Foo Foo by Michael Rosen (Walker Books, 2003)

Russell the Sheep by Rob Scotton (HarperCollins, 2005)

Mr Wolf's Pancakes by Jan Fearnley (Egmont Books, 1999)

Don't Worry!

by Christopher Stitt

Questions to ask and discussion ideas

Front cover
Read the title and the author's and illustrator's names. What do the children think the story might be about? Who might the characters be? Where might they live?

Pages 2 and 3
What is Gran worried about? What are the mice doing? Who does she tell?

What does her granddaughter say? How do you think she might do this?

Look at the picture on page 3. What room are they in? What time of day do you think it is? Why? What is Gran wearing? What do you think her granddaughter is eating?

Pages 4 and 5
How did the granddaughter get rid of the mice? What did she get?

What problem did the cats cause? What did the granddaughter say?

What do you think she might do to get rid of the cats?

Look at the picture. How many cats can you see? Where are they? What is Gran doing?

Pages 6 and 7
How did the granddaughter get rid of the cats? Why didn't Gran like the dogs? What did the granddaughter say?

How do you think the granddaughter will get rid of the dogs?

Look at the picture. How many dogs can you see? What are they doing? What has happened to the kitchen?

Pages 8 and 9
How did the granddaughter get rid of the dogs? What did the goats do to the dogs?

What did Gran say? What did the granddaughter say? How do you think she will do this? What would you do?

Look at the picture. How many goats can you see? What have they done?

Pages 10 and 11
What did the granddaughter get to get rid of the goats? Where do you think she got them from?

What did Gran say? What did her granddaughter say?

Look at the picture. How many tigers can you see? Where is Gran? What have the tigers done to the kitchen?

How do you think she will get rid of the tigers? What would you do?

Pages 12 and 13
What did she use to get rid of the tigers?

What did Gran say? What did the granddaughter say? How do you think she will get rid of the elephants?

Pages 14 and 15
What got rid of the elephants? What did the elephants do to Gran's house?

What do you think Gran will say now?

Page 16
Why do you think Gran decided she liked the mice after all?

Did you find the story funny? What parts did you think were funny?

Did you like the story? Why?

Name

Cut out the pictures.
Put them in order to tell the story of 'Don't Worry!'

Name

Choose a word from the box to complete each sentence.
Add a **?** to the end of each sentence.

1. ____________ did Gran want

2. ____________ got rid of the mice

3. ____________ did the goats go

4. ____________ you help me

5. ____________ do dogs hate cats

6. ____________ can I visit again

what	who
will	where
when	why

Complete these questions using your own ideas.
Remember the **?**

1. Why ____

2. When ____

3. Who ____

4. What ____

5. Where ____

6. Will ____

Name

Circle words that mean the same as those in bold.

like	hate	love	little	bike
screamed	said	laughed	yelled	sang
looked	ran	locked	jumped	peeped
nice	lovely	horrible	young	ice

Which word would you use? Write the sentence underneath.

1. I **love** my gran. I **enjoy** my gran.

____

2. These cakes are **good**. These cakes are **pleasant**.

____

3. The man **cried** at the dog. The man **yelled** at the dog.

____

4. I **looked** it up in a book. I **glanced** it up in a book.

____

5. I am **jolly** for you. I am **happy** for you.

____

Further activity ideas

Speaking and listening

- ❑ Use the story to begin a discussion about what the children find funny. What do they think is funny in this story? Why? Have they read another book that is funny? What is so funny about it? What makes them laugh?
- ❑ Have a joke day. Ask the children to find some jokes and bring them to school to share with others.
- ❑ Dramatise the play with the children acting all the parts, including the animals.
- ❑ Read and share other funny stories. Ask the children to bring in their favourite funny book. Make a class display of them.
- ❑ Sing animal songs.
- ❑ Talk about the animals in the story. Share ideas about where they live, what they eat and the kinds of things they do. Who has mice, cats or dogs as pets? What kinds of things do they get up to? Has anyone seen a goat, tiger, elephant? What were they like? Would an elephant really fit inside a house?
- ❑ Set up a role play area as a veterinary clinic or a zoo.
- ❑ Talk about the gran in the story. What was she like? What clothes did she wear? Share ideas about the children's own grans. Where do they live? How often do they see them? What are they like? What kinds of things do they do together? The children could bring in photos of their grans and share them with a friend or small group.
- ❑ The children could interview their grans. They could find out about their gran's life or they could ask their gran to tell them about what they were like before they went to school. What things can their gran tell them that their parents haven't?

Writing

- ❑ What happened to the elephants? Where did they go? Were they really frightened? Did they cause chaos? The children could write the story of the elephants.
- ❑ Ask the children to write about their grans. They could draw pictures, bring in photographs and make a book.
- ❑ Make a class joke book. Each child could write a joke and illustrate it. Put it in the school library for others to enjoy.
- ❑ Have fun with alliteration and tongue-twisters. What funny sentences can the children invent? For example:

  Peter picked a pickled possum.
  Seven slimy sausages sang silly songs.
  Fred Fish found five frilly fat frogs.
  Wiggly worms wibble and wobble.

- ❑ Invent spells for getting rid of things! How to get rid of younger brothers. How to get rid of bullies. How to get rid of rainy weather. How to get rid of your teacher!
- ❑ Ask the children to choose one of the animals in the story and find out more about it. They could make a poster for the wall or an information booklet.
- ❑ Make an animal alphabet. The children could use dictionaries to find animals for each letter of the alphabet. Can they get an animal for every letter?
- ❑ Write other stories about a gran. For example, 'The day my gran disappeared', 'My gran, the spy', 'Gran to the rescue' or 'Supergran'.

8. Finish the book blurb.

This story is about a boy called Tommy Tickle who liked to make people laugh. One day

____

____

______________________________________.

Read the story to find out what happened.

1. Colour the picture.
Write your name.

Tommy Tickle

by ________________________________

2. You are going to write a funny story about a boy called Tommy Tickle. Choose what Tommy likes to do:
   a. dress up in funny clothes
   b. tell jokes all the time

   Colour the picture and finish the sentence.

Tommy Tickle liked to make other people laugh. He would ______________________________

____.

7. Say how the story ends. Tommy gave up trying to make his friends laugh. He:
   a. became a famous TV comic
   b. joined the circus as a clown and travelled the world

   Colour the picture and finish the sentence.

From that day on Tommy decided never to make his friends laugh again. Instead he

____

____.

6. Say how the problem was solved. Tommy made everyone better by:
    a. tickling their funny bone
    b. inventing a special medicine

Draw the happy children. Finish the sentence.

But it was Tommy himself who found a cure for the children. He ____________________

____

and they all went back to how they were before.

3. Say what his friends were like. They:
    a. always wanted to play with him
    b. invited him to all their parties

Draw Tommy and his friends and finish the sentence.

Tommy Tickle had lots of friends. They all liked him very much. They ______________

____________________________________.

4. Give the story a problem. His friends laughed so much:

    a. they curled up into little balls and stayed that way

    b. their stomachs fell out and they couldn't eat any more

    Draw a picture. Write a sentence.

One day Tommy made his friends laugh so much that a terrible thing happened.

____

____

5. Say what the children's parents did. They:

    a. spent lots of money at the hospital trying to get a cure

    b. told their story to a newspaper, hoping someone could help

    Colour the picture and finish the sentence.

The children's parents were very upset. They

____

______________________________.

Tommy Tickle
Word bank

again	curled	medicine
angry	decided	newspaper
better	friends	parents
bone	happened	special
children	hospital	stomachs
circus	invited	terrible
clown	jokes	tickling
comic	laugh	travelled
cure	laughed	upset

My own words

The Dog Who Wanted to Fly
by ____________________

You are going to plan and write a funny story.
Use the information below to help you or use your own ideas.

The characters

Choose the characters for your story.

a) A dog who lived on a farm with the farmer and his wife

or

b) A dog who lived with the Brown family – mother, father and daughter, Sara, in a city house

Think of a funny name for the dog.

____

What did the dog do all day?

____

The beginning

How will your story begin?

One day the dog decides he wants to learn how to fly. The dog:

a) joins up for flying lessons at the local airport.

or

b) asks his friend, the robin, to show him what to do.

Why does the dog want to learn how to fly?

____

What do the dog's family think?

____

The middle

What happens?

The flying lessons all go wrong! The dog:

a) can only fly upside down so he keeps crashing into things and breaking them.

or

b) has a lot of trouble landing. He keeps sliding along the ground until he crashes into something.

How do the people feel about all their things being broken?

____

The end

What happens in the end?

The dog has to earn some money to pay for all the damage so he:

a) works in a restaurant, licking all the plates clean!

or

b) sells hot dogs at the market.

How does the dog feel about flying now?

____

The Dog Who Wanted to Fly
Word bank

airport	family	money
angry	flying	people
break	friend	restaurant
broke	landing	robin
broken	learn	sliding
crashed	lessons	trouble
damage	licking	upset
decided	lived	wanted
earn	market	

My own words

Unit 6

Adventure stories

Writers of adventure stories aim to enthral, excite and entertain the reader. To do this, they create a hero or heroine who is essentially 'good' from a moral perspective but who has no superhuman powers. The writer then places this character in an exciting situation, such as being challenged by a sinister villain or forced to do battle with the elements in a natural disaster of some kind.

Adventure stories are usually action-packed and just when the reader breathes a sigh of relief that the hero has managed to extricate himself from a perilous situation, another life-threatening emergency occurs. The reader is repeatedly left in suspense by a series of cliffhangers, wondering whether the hero will be able to overcome yet another obstacle. However, the conclusion of most adventure stories brings triumph for the hero or heroine over the adversity that he or she faced.

Adventure stories may be set in exotic locations or against a more mundane background with colourful villains, but they are always rooted in reality.

Common themes in adventure stories are:

- The indomitable capacity of the human spirit to reveal bravery when confronted with an ordeal of some kind.
- That separation from one's parents or the familiar leads to vulnerability.
- That insight and understanding can be gained from horrifying experiences.

Other frequent elements of adventure stories are an apparently secure setting or situation that lulls the reader into a false sense of security and death-defying escapes which take the form of a race or a chase.

A successful adventure story is the ultimate page-turner, which grips the reader with thrills and spills. Once finished, it leaves the reader with an enormous sense of satisfaction, almost a feeling of exhilaration!

Adventure stories

Examples of adventure stories

Dolphin Boy by Michael Morpurgo (Andersen Press, 2004)

Ben and Gran and the Whole, Wide, Wonderful World by Gillian Shields (Macmillan Children's, 2005)

Just for You! by Christine Leeson (Little Tiger Press, 2005)

The Giraffe and the Pelly and Me by Roald Dahl (Puffin, 2001)

Meet Just William – William's Haunted House and Other Stories by Richmal Crompton, adapted by Martin Jarvis (Macmillan, 1999)

Pirate Boy by John Wallace (Picture Lions, 2003)

Lost in the Park

by Roger Carr

Questions to ask and discussion ideas

Front cover
Read the title and the author's and illustrator's names. What do the children think the story might be about? Who might the characters be? What do you think may have caused them to get lost?

Pages 2 and 3
Who is Tom? Who is Mack? What do they like to do together? What sorts of adventures do you think they might have in the park? What do you think the park might be like?

What did Dad say to Tom? Why do you think he said this?

Pages 4 and 5
How did Tom and Mack get into the park? What sort of gates were they? What sort of park was it? What sorts of things were there in the park? What do you think Tom and Mack will do?

Have you been to a park? How did you get there? What was it like? What kinds of things were there? What did you do there?

Pages 6 and 7
Where did Tom and Mack go? What happened?

How did Tom feel? How would you feel if you were lost? What might Tom do? What would you do?

What do you think will happen next?

Look at the picture. What can you see? Where have you seen this picture before?

Pages 8 and 9
What did Tom do? Why do you think he called out?

Look at the picture. How does Tom look? How does Mack look?

Why do you think Mack pulled Tom's shoelace? What do you think Mack will do next?

Pages 10 and 11
How did Mack try to talk to Tom? What do you think he was trying to say?

Do any of you own a dog? Can your dog tell you things? What does it do to tell you it wants to go outside? Have a drink? Go for a walk?

Can animals know things that people don't?

Pages 12 and 13
What did Tom say to Mack? How do you think Mack knew the way to go back? Why don't dogs get lost as easily as people do?

Pages 14 and 15
What made Mack suddenly stop running? How did Tom feel?

What did Mack do? What happened?

Why do you think Tom's father came to the park? What do you think will happen next?

Page 16
What did Tom tell his Dad? How do you think Tom feels now? How do you think his Dad feels?

Do you think Tom will go to the park again?

How can we stay safe when we go to a park?

Name

Cut out the pictures.
Put them in order to tell the story of 'Lost in the Park'.

Name

Choose the correct word to complete each sentence.

1.	Mack barked and ____________ around.	**run**	**ran**
2.	Last week they __________ to the park.	**went**	**go**
3.	When they __________ to the gates they were open.	**come**	**came**
4.	No one _________ to help them.	**come**	**came**
5.	Mack _____________ at the snake.	**bark**	**barked**
6.	Tom ____________ after him.	**run**	**ran**

Write your own sentence for each word.

1. **came**

____

2. **went**

____

3. **barked**

____

4. **run**

____

5. **ran**

____

Name

Find the words in the puzzle. Circle each one.

p	a	t	h	r	t	p	f	w	i	l
s	p	r	i	k	r	h	o	f	v	m
q	a	c	l	b	a	g	r	a	s	s
b	d	o	l	m	c	n	k	b	k	n
i	o	k	s	a	k	r	b	e	u	a
r	t	i	l	g	s	k	c	x	d	k
d	z	n	p	f	o	r	e	s	t	e
s	h	p	a	r	k	c	b	y	r	u
s	d	y	f	l	i	q	f	b	e	h
a	f	g	x	b	u	g	a	t	e	s
a	n	i	m	a	l	s	f	p	s	w

forest
grass
snake
path
trees
animals
hills
birds
park
tracks
fork
gates

Use words from the puzzle to complete the sentences.

Tom and Mack liked going to the p________________. The park g______________ were at the end of the street. The park was a f_______________ park. It had lots of little p_______________ that led to secret places. There were a__________________ and b_______________ in the park. There were h_______________ and t__________________.

Further activity ideas

Speaking and listening

- Use the story to begin a discussion about being lost. Have any of the children ever been lost? Where? How old were they? How did they feel? What did they do? What happened? What can we do if we get lost in a supermarket? Shopping centre? Street? How can we make sure we stay safe?

  You could develop this further by inviting the police schools' liaison officer into the classroom to talk to the children about staying safe.

- Discuss how we can tell people things without using words. Talk about how the dog 'tells' the boy what to do. How do babies tell us what they need? Have the children ever seen someone using sign language? You could teach them some simple alphabet signs using a website such as: www.british-sign.co.uk or www.learnbsl.org

- Talk about pets and how they can help us. What do those children who have pets enjoy about them? How do they take care of them? What things should we do to keep our pets safe and healthy? The children could bring along a picture of their pets and talk about them.

- Talk about the parks near your school. What things are there? What can you do in the park? What things could be improved? This could lead to the children writing a letter to the local council if action is needed!

- What sounds might Tom and Mack hear in the park? Can the children make the sound of a snake? An owl? A robin? Leaves rustling in the trees? The dog barking? The sound of footsteps on the path? This could develop into a guessing game where the children make the sound of an animal for others to guess what it is.

Writing

- The children could write their own story about being lost. It might be something that actually happened to them or something imaginary.

- Make a class book about keeping safe. The children could draw pictures and write about how to stay safe at home, at school, in the park or on the street, following a class discussion about the things to remember.

- Find out about animals who help us, such as seeing and hearing dogs. How do these dogs help the hard of hearing and those with impaired sight? How are the dogs trained? You could invite someone from the Guide Dogs for the Blind organisation to talk to the children. The children could prepare some questions to ask them. They could make posters to encourage people to donate to the charity.

- The children could practise writing their full name and address so they know what to write if they actually do get lost!

- Make a map of the school or local area. Mark an 'x' on a spot. Tell the children that the 'x' is where someone is who is lost. He can't find his way back to ... (the school, the classroom). Can the children write directions for how to get there?

- Find out about National Parks in Britain. Look at maps showing where they are located. Have the children ever visited any of them? Talk about how we should behave in these places – not dropping any litter, closing gates, using only designated paths and so on. The children could write a set of rules for keeping the countryside a nice place to be in.

- Ask the children to think of words to describe their own park (or school grounds if there is no park nearby). They can include items in the park. Challenge them to make their own wordsearch using these words.

8. Finish the book blurb.

This story is about a girl called Natasha who liked to walk along the cliff path. One day she

____

____.

Read the story to find out what happened.

Unit 6 – Scaffold 1

1. Colour the picture.
   Write your name.

Cliff Rescue

by ________________________________

2. You are going to write an adventure story about a girl called Natasha. Choose where she lives:

a. in a caravan

b. in a house on a cliff

Colour the picture and finish the sentence.

Natasha lives in a ______________________

______________________.

She loves to go walking near the sea.

7. Say how the story ends. The rescue team arrive. They:

a. use a helicopter to lift her out

b. climb down on ropes and carry her up

Colour the picture and finish the sentence.

Soon the rescue team arrived. They ________

______________________.

Natasha was cold and tired but at last she was safe!

6. Say how the problem was solved. A man hears her. He was:

   a. walking his dog

   b. going to visit a friend

Draw the man finding Natasha. Finish the sentence.

A man who was ____________________ ____________________ heard Natasha. He ran over and shouted down to her. "Don't worry. I'll call the police," he said.

3. Say what she does on her walks. Natasha:

   a. collects brightly coloured seashells

   b. picks up driftwood and fossils

Draw Natasha on a walk and finish the sentence.

On her walks, Natasha likes to ____________ ____________________________.

She takes them home with her.

4. Give the story a problem. Walking along a cliff path she:

    a. slipped and fell down the cliff, landing on a ledge

    b. walked away from the path and fell down an old mine

Colour the picture. Finish the sentence.

One day Natasha was walking along the cliff path when she ______________________

______________________________________.

She cried out but no one could hear her.

5. Say what happened next. It began to get dark. Natasha:

    a. kept calling out, hoping someone would hear her

    b. sang songs to herself to stop feeling frightened

Draw a picture and finish the sentence.

Soon it began to get dark and Natasha was afraid. She ______________________

____

______________________________________.

Cliff Rescue
Word bank

afraid
arrived
caravan
cliff
collects
cried
fossils
friend
frightened
helicopter
helped
house
ledge
rescue
safely
seashells
shouted
slipped
someone
stretcher
tired
unhurt
walking
worried

My own words

Zoo Disaster

by ____________________

You are going to plan and write an adventure story.
Use the information below to help you or use your own ideas.

The characters

Choose the characters for your story.

a) A boy, his brother and his mum

or

b) A boy and his grandad

Think of a name for the boy.

____

Where does he live?

____

The beginning

How will your story begin?

One day the characters go to the zoo. The boy is really excited because he wants to see:

a) the monkeys playing on their swings.

or

b) the lions prowling and roaring.

What do they do when they first arrive?

____

The boy is very naughty. He tries to open the gates to where the animals live.

The middle

What happens?

The boy opens one of the gates!

a) A rhino gets out and chases the boy.

or

b) A lion gets out and chases the boy.

The boy is very frightened.
What does the boy do? Where does he run to?

____

What happens to the other people at the zoo?

____

The end

What happens in the end?

The zookeepers:

a) dart the animal to put it to sleep. They carry it back before it wakes up.

or

b) capture the animal in a giant net and return it.

The zookeepers rescue the boy. What do they say to him?

____

What does the boy decide to do?

____

Zoo Disaster
Word bank

animals	everywhere	rescue
arrived	excited	return
brother	frightened	rhino
capture	hiding	roaring
chaos	lion	running
chased	monkeys	zookeeper
decides	naughty	
enclosure	people	
escaped	prowling	

My own words